Christian, are you living
in orbit or out of orbit?
Are you suffering
from "spiritual heartburn"?
Are you really resting in the Lord,
or are you just rusting in yourself?
Are you content
with "barnyard security"
when you ought to be soaring
in the skies?
Perhaps you have not discovered
the true cycle of victorious living
in Christ. Within these pages,
Earl G. Lee tells how you too can
be *RECYCLED for Living*.

Earl G. Lee

Recycled for Living

COMMIT COMMIT COMMIT COMMIT COMMIT COMMIT COMMIT COMMIT COMMIT COMMIT

REST REST REST
REST REST REST
REST REST REST
REST REST REST
REST REST REST

TRUST TRUST TR
TRUST TRUST TR
TRUST TRUST TR
TRUST TRUST TR
TRUST TRUST TR

DELIGHT DELIGHT DELIGHT DELIGHT DELIGHT DELIGHT DELIGHT DELIGHT DELIGHT DELIGHT

G/L REGAL BOOKS

A Division of G/L Publications
Glendale, California, U.S.A.

The Authorized Version (King James) is the biblical basis for this book. Superior numbers used with Scripture verses quoted in this text refer to these other Bibles.

[1] *The Living Bible*, Paraphrased. (Taylor) Wheaton: Tyndale House, Publishers, 1971. Used by permission.

[2] *The New Testament in Modern English*. (Phillips) New York: the Macmillan Company, 1958. Used by permission.

[3] *The Amplified Bible*. Grand Rapids: Zondervan Publishing House, 1965. Used by permission.

[4] *The Berkeley Version in Modern English*. Grand Rapids: Zondervan Publishing House, 1969. Used by permission.

[5] *The New Testament, A New Translation*. (Moffatt) New York: Harper and Row Publishers, Inc. 1964. Used by permission.

[6] *The New English Bible: New Testament.* © The Delegates of the Oxford University Press and the Syndics of the Cambridge University Press 1961, 1970. Reprinted by permission.

[7] Young's Literal Translation of the Bible, 1862.

Second Printing, 1974

Published by
Regal Books Division, G/L Publications
Glendale, California 91209
Library of Congress Catalog Card No. 72-94753
ISBN 0-8307-0217-2

Second Edition

Originally published under the title *The Cycle of Victorious Living*.

Contents

Dedication

*To those who have meant the most to me
in my walk with Christ and its development:
My wife, Hazel
My children, Gary, Gayle, and Grant*

Appreciation is expressed to Gert Behenna for permission to quote from her book "The Late Liz," in chapter one. To "Guideposts" for permission to use the poem by Toki Miyashina, called "23rd Psalm for Busy People," in chapter five.

Foreword

Never so many people on earth as now! And never so few, comparatively, who believe in *life!*

They are not confident of life because they are not committed to Life: "I am the way, the truth, and the life" (John 14:6). As one of them put it, pathetically, "The only thing I wanted out of life was to get out of it." He wanted escape, not engagement. Engagement means to be *geared in, involved, going ahead.*

Earl Lee writes as a man who, having found life in Christ, has gone on to a level of living on which four insights of the Thirty-Seventh Psalm have focused a steady and a steadying light. In this modest "testament of devotion" his primary interest is not to enunciate a doctrine but to describe a style of life. Simple, straightforward words are the vehicles on which the author's outgoing, pastoral concern comes through to the reader—helpfully, as I believe.

Paul S. Rees

Fret not thyself because of evildoers, neither be thou envious against the workers of iniquity.

For they shall soon be cut down like the grass, and wither as the green herb.

Trust in the Lord, and do good; so shalt thou dwell in the land, and verily thou shalt be fed.

Delight thyself also in the Lord; and he shall give thee the desires of thine heart.

Commit thy way unto the Lord; trust also in him; and he shall bring it to pass.

And he shall bring forth thy righteousness as the light, and thy judgment as the noonday.

Rest in the Lord, and wait patiently for him: fret not thyself because of him who prospereth in his way, because of the man who bringeth wicked devices to pass.

Psalm 37:1-7

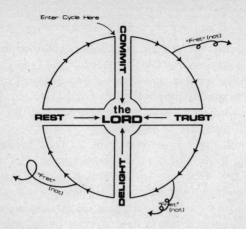

Preface

While on deputation work after my second term as a missionary in India I entered into a new level of life in the Spirit. Due to the nudging of the Spirit, I knew before I left India that I would not be returning for a third term. This revelation was extremely jolting for two reasons: I loved India and she had become a satisfying way of life for me; also, facing a new direction in my middle years was not easy. As our ship drew away from India's shores I can still see a fellow missionary making the sign of the cross with her hands. Little did she know how appropriate was her farewell.

"What are your plans for the future?" was the question I faced repeatedly during those deputation days. I tried to explain the unusual direction of the Spirit's guidance in my life, but people's baffled looks added to my increasing frustration. It did not make sense—and I became a bit desperate in my spirit.

During the month of October, 1960, while on a missionary tour in Oklahoma, I told the Lord I needed a settled spirit, a sure promise. The answer I received was so quietly simple I hardly knew God had spoken. His word to me was, "You *have* My will for today; I will take care of tomorrow."

I felt great inner relaxation as God brought my living to its least common denominator. His will for the day! That was all that was necessary. Although it would be over nine months before I was to have any idea what the future held for me and my family, I had entered into a new level of living, much like ships go from one lock to another in a canal. It was a move upward in my spirit, and the truths which came to me through this experience I have called *the cycle of victorious living.*

Although this fresh insight could have come to me through the writings of Paul or the teachings of Christ, it opened up to me through the Thirty-Seventh Psalm.

In order to clarify the truth, I have devised the diagram below. A glance at it shows the smooth sequence of living in a spiritual orbit. *Fret* is always the way out of orbit. With a bit of change of scriptural sequence we stay in the cycle by *committing, trusting, delighting,* and finally *resting.* Jesus Christ is the great Center of victorious living. The phrase "in the Lord" is the key thought. As I try to explain these truths more fully in the following chapters, I trust many will enter into a new level of dynamic, Spirit-filled life in Christ.

CHAPTER ONE

Fret Not

I was asked recently by a religious organization to speak on the subject of victorious living. Due to a printer's error, the subject was announced as "The Cycle of *Victorian* Living." I was quite amused as I read the card. No, it is not *Victorian* living. It is not a life of continual negatives, prohibitions, inhibitions, and long-faced unimpressiveness. People who live out their lives "in quiet desperation" are a part of the problem of religious life today rather than a part of the solution. They fret. God wants us to be free from continual fretting. We need to unravel some of the tangles in our thinking and realize how completely free God wants us to be. He has made provision for abundant living through the power of the Holy Spirit in the fully yielded heart.

He is not teasing us when He tells us not to fret, but it is quite possible that there is some confusion as to the meaning of the word *fret*. What one may call "fret" others may call "legitimate concern," or the opposite may be true. Yet it is amazing how the Holy Spirit can guide us through a maze of semantics into vital truth. He does not wish our spiritual life to become frayed no matter how we interpret words. *Fret not* is more than a pastoral platitude; it is a divine imperative.

Now David faced a legitimate concern. You would think he had access to one of our daily newspapers as he wrote about the ungodly prospering and evil-doers standing in the way of the righteous. His psalms are full of these observations. But his opening admonition in Psalm 37 is *"Fret not."*

In writing to the Philippians, Paul said, "Be careful for nothing" (4:6). Or, as *The Living New Testament* translates it, "Don't worry about anything; instead, pray about everything; tell God your needs and don't forget to thank him for his answers. If you do this you will experience God's peace, which is far more wonderful than the human mind can understand. His peace will keep your thoughts and your hearts quiet and at rest as you trust in Christ Jesus" (Phil. 4:6,7). Over and over again, we are pointed to the great Center, Christ Jesus.

Paul did not write these words from the Huntington-Sheraton Hotel. He was in jail. But the entire letter to the Philippians sounds like Paul had found his cycle of victorious living while in a dungeon. He uses such phrases as "Be careful for nothing"; "I trust in the Lord"; "I can do all things through Christ"; "Rejoice in the Lord alway"; "The God of peace shall be with you"; "I have all, and abound"; "My God shall supply all your need"; "I have learned, in whatsoever state I am, therewith to be content"; "Now unto God and our Father be glory for ever and ever" (Phil. 4:6; 2:24; 4:13; 4:4; 4:9; 4:18; 4:19; 4:11; 4:20).

The teachings of Jesus have the same familiar ring. "Seek ye first the kingdom of God"; "Take . . . no thought for the morrow"; "Lay up for yourselves treasures in heaven"; "Consider the lilies of the field"; "Ask, and it shall be given you; seek, and ye shall find; knock, and it shall be opened unto you" (Matt. 6:33,34; 6:20,28; 7:7).

Oswald Chambers says, "All our fret and worry is caused by calculating without God." It destroys victorious living as surely as insects and other pests destroy leaves.

I enjoy caring for my roses, camellias, and azaleas. I had one very anemic camellia bush off in a corner of the flower bed. Weeds had sprung up around it and, although it gave a few weak blooms, I determined to restore its beauty. As I cleaned out the weeds, I discovered the true cause for concern. Embedded in the soil near the roots and on up under the leaves were a number of well-fed snails. I heartily disliked their intrusion and decided then and there they would have to go if I was to have a healthy camellia bush. With the use of specially prepared pellets they were done away with. The blooms have been rich and colorful ever since.

Fret is the snail under the leaf, and in order to have lives of fragrance and beauty, these snails of fret must go. And God has a specially prepared way for their exit. It is found in the cycle of victorious living!

Tension is normal and natural in life. Without tension we could not exist any more than a violin string can be played without being stretched across the bridge. This creative tension is not the same thing as destructive worry. Worry is like racing an automobile engine while it is in neutral. The gas and noise and smog do not get us anywhere. But legitimate concern (creative tension) is putting the car into low gear on your way to moving ahead. You tell yourself that you are going to use the power God has given you to do something about the situation which could cause you to fret.

One really moves into high gear when he affirms, "Now unto him that is able to do exceeding abundantly above all that we ask or think, according to the power that worketh in us, unto him be glory" (Eph. 3:20,21). That Scripture goes places, and you go with it. It's a long way from worrying, fretting, and stewing in a state of paralysis. Maybe you are like me. When I know there is something that needs to be done, or someone I need to see, I am miserable until I take care of the matter. Fret usually is not removed by praying, but by doing. One has to take the gear shift out of neutral, put it into "low," and get going.

Dr. E. Stanley Jones told about a bird in India which he called a champion pessimist. This bird goes around all day crying shrilly, "Pity-to-do-it, pity-to-do-it," and at night, they say, he sleeps on his back with his long legs in the air to keep the sky from falling!

Too often we excuse ourselves by saying, "Well, I'm just a natural worrywart!" But let me tell you, if you examine the worrywart you will find its malady is malignant. It eats down into the spirit until it destroys life. The only way to handle this critical malignancy is to let the Holy Spirit operate on it—because FRET TAKES US OUT OF ORBIT. It is the cell malfunctioning, refusing to work with the normal, happily functioning body cells. It has become self-centered and its refusal to cooperate can bring death. The symptom must be treated speedily and faced with a ruthless honesty. There can be no amateur approach to this deep need. It takes a specialist to handle a malignancy, and the Holy Spirit is the Great Specialist. But He can operate only on the yielded spirit, and the anesthetic is grace.

Someone has described fret as "spiritual heartburn." Most of us can understand that description. Here is a dictionary definition for fret: "To eat away, to gnaw, to gall, to vex, to worry, to agitate, to wear away." As Jesus tells us, "The worries of the world . . . come in to choke the word"[5] (Mark 4:19).

I have made my own acrostic definition for the word fret. It is:

*F*ear
*R*esentment
*E*nvy
*T*ension (destructive)

Sometimes Charlie Brown can be quite a theologian. In one cartoon we see Linus dragging his blanket as he observes, "You look kinda' depressed, Charlie Brown."

Charlie replies, "I worry about school a lot." Then he adds, "I worry about my worrying so much about school." As they sit on a log together, Charlie makes his final observation: "My anxieties have anxieties!"

After I used this illustration about Charlie Brown in one of my Sunday sermons, I received the following letter:

"Dear Pastor Lee,

I want to say, Praise the Lord, while it is fresh in my heart. I have been troubled by a verse for some time now. *The New English Bible* in Phil. 4:6 says, 'The Lord is near; have no anxiety, but in everything make your requests known to God in prayer and petition with thanksgiving.'[6] God knows that I have been torn by anxiety over insignificant things. Your quote from Snoopy about worrying about worry seemed to fit me. Your message on *Fret Not* was for me. I placed all my worrying and fretting on the altar and left it there, glory be to God! I now claim the above verse, for I have come to realize that it is the second part, 'with thanksgiving' and praise, that makes the first part reality.

In Christ,"

Naturally, this letter warmed my heart. It is a deep thrill when the sheep go into greener pastures. How wonderful to realize that "all God's commandments are enablings"! Our heavenly Father never asks us to do what He does not help us, through His grace, to do. It is a loving, providing Father who says, "Don't fret." He wants us to move up into more abundant living above the smog-filled atmosphere of fret.

I am not proposing an impossible way of life. I am not saying one will never fret. But I do maintain there is a cycle of victorious living, a working in and a working out of 1 Corinthians, chapter 13, whereby life ever has an upbeat. When we realize we are becoming victims of fret, that we are getting out of orbit, we ask forgiveness and get back into the cycle by once more committing our way unto the Lord.

CHAPTER TWO

Commit

David says, "Commit thy way unto the Lord; trust also in him; and he shall bring it to pass" (Ps. 37:5). Or as Robert Young translates it, "He worketh."[7]

David also adds, "He shall bring forth thy righteousness as the light, and thy judgment as the noonday" (Ps. 37:6).

It all starts with commitment.

Commitment is something other than a sentimental decision that may change one's life for a few emotion-filled days. It is a valid act of the will changing one's whole way of life. It is one's entrance into the cycle of victorious living.

The true meaning of the word *commit* came to me as I was reading this passage in Marathi, our "stepmother" tongue of India. If I were to make a free translation of the Marathi, it says, "Turn what you are and what you have over to God—palms down!"

9

Suppose I hold a piece of chalk in my hand and ask you to take it. You reach out and take it from my upturned hand. But commitment means that we turn our palms over and completely drop what we hold. Nothing of it sticks to our hands.

This process involves an exercise of the will. It reminds me of Oswald Chambers' words, "I have nothing to do with what will happen if I obey. I must abandon myself to God's call in unconditional surrender and smilingly wash my hands of the consequences."

This prayer goes beyond "You take it" to "I release it." There's quite a difference. It is the prayer I made that day in Oklahoma when I entered into a new level of Spirit-filled living.

Commitment is both initial and continuous. We enter the cycle by commitment. The need, the problem, the urgent prayer request are all given over to God. But one's mind remains quite active, and here is where Satan comes in to accuse. He has not been called "the accuser of the brethren" for nothing! Whenever the temptation to fret assails us, we must tell our adversary that the bothersome matter is now in God's hands and he is wasting his time in needling us.

Satan is not omniscient; he has to be told that we mean business. "Resist the devil, and he will flee" (James 4:7). Send him to your great Advocate, Jesus Christ. Jesus knows the set of your heart, the direction of your will, and He also knows how to protect you and how to help you handle your emotions.

The will has often been likened to the rudder of a boat. But have you thought of how much more boat there is than rudder? Our emotions make up most of our conscious being, but, as Archbishop Fenelon of Cambrai said, our will to obey God is where true religion resides.

If I were being troubled by someone who was out to destroy my reputation and I had placed my case in the hands of a competent lawyer, I would not waste time talking to my adversary; I would speedily refer him to my lawyer. When you are tempted to relive all the pre-commitment days, the pain and the struggle, and feel the slight edge of doubt moving in, remember the telephone number of your Advocate and put in your call, "Thank You, Lord . . . I believe!"

I like William Osterly's translation of the Hebrew for *commit*. He says, "It takes on the idea of to roll, whirl, turn . . . the wholehearted flinging of one's self upon God, knowing that *His will prevails.*"

I was interested in reading about Dr. J. Edwin Orr's experience in commitment. As he was struggling to be filled with the Spirit, he prayed, "Now, Lord, I will give You my business." Nothing happened.

As he was also in the throes of making a decision concerning a life's companion, he added, "Lord, I will give her to You." Still nothing happened.

One day, in desperation, he cried, "Lord, I give You my choice of a career." Still nothing happened.

Finally he completely let go and prayed, "Lord, I give You myself. I commit to You my will and You have *me.*" Then the Holy Spirit came in cleansing power.

True commitment means we wash our hands of ourselves and give to Him our all—totally, not on condition. When conditions are attached, our palms are held upward; but deep commitment means our *palms are down*. It is the only way to enter the cycle of victorious living. It demands faith in the character of our God and not in the circumstances we see or understand. Oswald Chambers reminds us that we command what we understand.

But, as has been stated, commitment is not only initial, it is continuous. We are human beings, not pieces of crystal. We face new situations constantly, and over and over new problems are fed into the cycle. But the process, once learned, becomes a glorious way of life. New light comes and specific areas are dealt with. You never "arrive" or cease to learn and apply principles of victory. This is practical, sanctified living.

I came across an illustration of commitment in a newspaper back in 1964. A man by the name of Robert Atwood wrote an article for the *Daily Times* of Anchorage, Alaska, describing the terrible earthquake which occurred on Good Friday of that year. He arrived home from work about 5:30 in the evening as his wife was leaving for the grocery store. He hesitated a moment as he considered going with her, but decided to remain home and practice his trumpet, as the house would be empty. (Not a bad idea for people who blow trumpets!) Now, in Mr. Atwood's words:

"I began practicing my trumpet when the earthquake started. Minor earthquakes are not uncommon here, but they've always taught me to stop what I'm doing and watch what happens. It was quickly obvious that this was no minor earthquake. The chandelier, made from a ship's wheel, swayed too much. Things were falling that had never fallen before. I headed for the door carrying my trumpet. At the door I saw a wall weaving. On the driveway I turned and watched my house swerve and groan as though in mortal agony. It was as though someone had engaged it in a gigantic taffy pull—stretching it, shrinking and twisting it. I became aware of tall trees falling in our yard, so I moved to a spot that I thought would be safe. As I moved I saw cracks appear in the earth. Pieces of ground in jigsaw shapes moved up and down, tilted at all angles.

As I started to climb the fence to my neighbor's yard, the fence disappeared. Trees were falling in crazy patterns. Deep chasms cushioned the impact. I was on the verge of a quick burial. I could not pull my right arm from the sand. It was buried to the shoulder. Most of the rest of my body was also covered. *I had to let go of my trumpet* and my arm pulled free easily!"

That story got to me. Too often our trumpets are the expression of our rights, our egos, our desire for recognition and reward; but when we commit our way, we commit ourselves and thus we learn to live without trumpets. "Take my yoke upon you, and learn of me; for I am meek and lowly in heart: and ye shall find rest unto your souls" (Matt. 11:29).

It may take an earthquake upheaval to pry us loose from our trumpets, but it is the only way that will lead to rest of soul.

A short time ago I was working with a weeping seeker at the altar. After a few moments she confessed that her mother was hindering her in her newly discovered way of life. I had preached recently on the cycle of victorious living and asked her if she had heard the sermon. She answered a faint, "Yes."

"Do you believe it?" I asked.

"Yes, Pastor, I do," was her reply.

"Then, Betty, I believe what you have to do is to commit your mother, as she is now, to the Lord. Place her in His hands without any condition. Then leave her there. Will you do this?"

I saw a light break over her drawn face as she answered, "I will do just that—now!"

After her prayer I reminded her that the Lord was in charge of her mother and she herself should begin to delight in the Lord and rest.

She began to thank the Lord right there and left the altar having stepped into the cycle.

I met her a week later and she said to me, "Believe me, delighting in the Lord was the way for me and my sister to live with my mother!"

It works! And it begins with commitment. The call to commitment is not from any man. It is God's call to us. His call is always total. He does not deal in partial victories nor will He be able to do much with half-hearted surrenders. Trumpets have to go. Palms have to be turned down and fully opened.

Elizabeth Burns (nee Gert Behanna), in the story of her life, *The Late Liz*, writes about her son, Allen, who rejected her long before she became a Christian and who refused all of her overtures after her conversion. He had caused her much heartache. She had wept over him far into the night and she wondered if God could ever bring all the pieces together. She writes:

"Like it or not, the day came when you bent over, swept up the pieces, glued them together, and took it from there. You yourself were a matter of what you did with the pieces.

"If this was true of me, it was true of my son as well. If it tore the heart out, the weight of Allen had to be lifted. The sorrow of him and of the harm I'd done him were blocks on the road to usefulness. Lift him up and let him go, *let him go.* Even if he was still alive, I still had to let him go. Allen's outcome was Allen's business. Grief could no longer block me from forgiving myself in order that I might learn to forgive all. 'So, son, you are released! My love pries you loose. My love hands you over to Him who is the Source of comfort.' "

She closes this experience with a strange statement, filled with keen insight, "I ached with the loss of my grief."

Where love is involved, where loved ones tear at the heart, the prayer of commitment often includes the prayer of relinquishment. It must have been that type of prayer that Abraham prayed as he climbed the mountain with his son and promised heir. It is one of the most difficult prayers we pray: "Lord, here it is; Lord, here he [or she] is; Lord, here I am; You have me." It is the only way into the cycle.

The illustration of a cycle is simply another approach to the words of Jesus in John 15:4, "Abide in me, and I in you. As the branch cannot bear fruit of itself, except it abide in the vine; no more can ye, except ye abide in me." It is a cycle of abiding.

CHAPTER THREE

Trust

"Pastor, I have really committed everything, including myself, to the Lord. Now what do I do?"

"There is only one thing to do, lean hard! You have changed from independence to dependence. You don't just lean; you lean on Someone well able to carry your weight, the One who created the heavens and the earth and who never fails."

The smile of understanding made me realize another one had entered into the cycle.

Trust is a key word in the Psalms. It is the word that weaves in and out of the cycle. "Trust in the Lord and do good; inhabit the land and practice faithfulness"[1] (Ps. 37:3).

The Amplified Bible translates the word for trust as "lean on, rely on, and be confident." I like to link that definition with the words of David Livingstone, who for the thousandth time placed his finger on the text on which he literally staked his life—"Lo,

I am with you alway, even unto the end of the world" (Matt. 28:20). Then, on the evening of January 14, 1856 he wrote in his diary, "It is the word of a gentleman of the most strict and sacred honor, so there's an end of it!"

This immensely lonely man, dying on his knees, left a last entry in his journal, "He will keep His word, the Gracious One, full of grace and truth; no doubt about it. He will keep His word, and it will be all right. Doubt is here inadmissible, surely!" God kept His sacred pledge.

If faith is nothing apart from its object, the same is true of trust, for they are closely akin in meaning. The recommendation from Scripture is to lean hard on the Lord. He made heaven and earth. He calms the storms and stills the waves. His is the earth "and the fulness thereof; the world, and they that dwell therein" (Ps. 24:1).

He is the One on whom you lean. All your weight on all of Him! You feel lighter after casting your cares on the Lord. Once you find release through commitment and trust, leaning hard becomes another forward move in the cycle. Here is meaningful, sanctified living, filled with adventure.

Recently I saw an interesting advertisement for a financial concern. They called on the public to take a realistic view of making out wills, and offered the services of their Trust Department. Their ad closed with these words, "Trust us. After all, *Trust* is a very important part of our name" (Commerce Bank and Trust Company). Would God not say that to us? "Trust is a very important part of My name."

This call of God requires an active response. We

do not place our trust in God and sit back and do nothing. A very important part of this transaction is expressed in the words of Mary, "Whatsoever he saith unto you, do it" (John 2:5). The result then was that the water was turned into wine. But the waterpots had to be filled first.

The Bible says for us to "trust . . . and do good." Doing good, having an obedient spirit, is an absolute necessity. We are freed from our burden, not to sit down, but to run with patience the race set before us. One cannot run entangled in cumbersome cares.

I am sure you realize it is possible anywhere along life's journey for fret to set in. Satan will not cease his efforts to get us out of orbit. He usually attacks the mind and seeks to insert insidious little doubts that, if allowed to, will easily start us toward fret. God's call for us not to fret is not only a requirement for entering the cycle but also a requirement for remaining in it. The opportunity to fret will always present itself; but as trust becomes more and more our way of life, we become less aware of the assaults on our faith.

I remember very vividly how easily I could have slipped out of the cycle of victorious living as I faced a staggering problem in one of my pastorates. First a pall of concern—good, legitimate concern—settled over my spirit. It was not long before I sensed that this concern was becoming seeded with fear. The clouds lowered over my spirit and I moved into a grey world. In my praying I was telling the Lord everything He already knew. I was actually making my apprehension verbal and getting mighty close to a condition of fret.

21

After about two days of such suffering, as I was driving to the church one morning, God "climbed" into the car beside me.

"Who asked you to come to this church in the first place?" He asked.

"Why, You did, Lord," I replied.

"Well, then all you need to do is to obey Me one step at a time. Give Me the problem and do as I say. This church does not belong to you; it belongs to Me!"

I rolled each care over on Him. Thanking Him for His faithful reminder to me that I was getting out of orbit, I found thanksgiving filling my heart.

It was the same process I followed back in 1960 while on that deputation tour. But it was a new situation, so the continuous process went on. Incidentally, need I add, the problem was gloriously taken care of, beyond all I could ask or think. Moffatt translates Psalm 37:5, "Leave all to him, rely on him, and he will see to it."[5] And that is exactly what He did.

There is a little chapel in Basim, India, which has a special significance to me. As resident missionary, I was responsible for the supervision of its construction in 1950 and soon after its completion our youngest son was dedicated at its altar by Dr. C. Warren Jones, at that time the retired foreign missions secretary.

One very hot day I stood at a distance watching the master mason do his work. Each stone was carefully fitted into place and many hands were required to complete the job. About a dozen coolies shuffled past me carrying head loads of crushed rock, which were handed up a shaky scaffold to the mason who properly mixed the cement and worked it around the larger, specially dressed stones. I did not realize the importance of the coolies until the Lord and I had a conversation.

"How closely you watch the master mason!" He said.

"Yes, Lord. He is an artist and his work is fascinating."

"But you have paid no attention to the coolies shuffling along beside you, have you?"

I was taken aback a bit as I said, "Coolies? Yes, but what they are doing doesn't interest me like the skilled work of the mason." (Yet there could be no work done in a land like India without them.)

Then He got all of my attention as the lesson He was teaching me came through: "Son, you are nothing but a coolie in My work. I am the Master Mason. Keep on handing Me what I need and I will see that the Kingdom is built."

How many times since that hot day have I reminded myself that I am nothing but a coolie. And again the deep meaning of the phrase in verse 5 burned into my spirit, "Trust . . . and he shall bring it to pass."

Paul expressed the same thought in a familiar Scripture, "I planted, Apollos watered, but God [all the while] was making it grow, and [He] gave the increase"[3] (1 Cor. 3:6).

CHAPTER FOUR

Delight

The clouds hung low that year in India. My wife and infant son were ill and the heavens were as brass with no apparent penetration. We were pressed beyond measure. One hot, still morning my wife came to me with the baby in her arms and said, "Take care of him for a while; I must find my way through this darkness. I am going to pray and not return until I have found an answer."

Her experience is best expressed in these words she wrote afterward:

"I closed the door and knelt down by the bed and cried out my heart's agony, 'O God, show me the way through, for I have no way to turn!'

As I waited, a quiet voice spoke to me, 'Look on the table beside the bed. You'll see the answer there.'

I was a bit startled but arose and walked over to the little night table. A small book lay on the table and the title, in letters of fire, read, *Rejoice.* Then God spoke to me again, saying, 'Here is the way through; praise Me and delight in Me for Myself alone, and I will come to your rescue.'

It sounds easy when one writes it, but to practice praise under those circumstances took a bit of re-thinking. I had been so consumed by the pressures of the problem, as well as extreme physical weakness, that to be able to express joy seemed an impossibility.

As I knelt again to pray, I was reminded by the Lord of my grandmother. My grandparents gave over twenty years of their lives as missionaries in the north of India. During the latter years of her life my grand-mother came to live with my mother. I loved her dearly and enjoyed talking to her about her many experiences as a missionary. She was afflicted with severe attacks of asthma. Many times I heard the sound of her thin little voice in the early morning, gasping out between painful wheezings, 'Praise the Lord! Hallelujah! Glory to God!'

One morning, as I took her breakfast tray to her, I was deeply upset and I asked rather exasperatedly, 'Grandma, what do you have to praise the Lord for? Why are you using your strength like this?' To my young mind things did not add up.

She smiled as she looked at me and said, 'I praise God for who He is, not for what comes into my life! I guess you would call it the sacrifice of praise. It brings peace to my heart and makes the suffering easier to bear.'

Now many years later, far away in a foreign land, the memory returned to me and the great lesson it taught. The sacrifice of praise—how wonderful!

After asking forgiveness, I began to praise the Lord with a heart filled with gratitude for all *He was to me.* Soon the brassy heavens began to melt and a shower of glory fell around my soul and the clouds of depression and darkness vanished into the sunlight of His presence."

As my wife shared this experience with me, we both turned a corner into a new way of life. It was the way of *purposeful delight.*

The Psalmist also reminds us that if we delight in the Lord we shall have the desires of our hearts. What desires? It is rather miraculous how delighting in God purifies these desires! Try it and you will discover for yourself what I mean.

We find the New Testament equivalent in Philippians 4:4, "Rejoice in the Lord alway: and again I say, Rejoice."

This great truth of delighting in the Lord is one which Satan continually tries to blur, and I would want to make it not only brighter in our thinking, but sharper in outline. For I believe here is where we have a deep problem in our cycle. Too often we forget to rejoice in the Lord. It is a matter of remembering to say, "Thank You." It means we revere the Giver more than His gift.

Once again I want to use an acrostic for a definition. To me, delighting in the Lord means:

*D*aily
*E*verything
*L*aid
*I*nto
*G*od's
*H*ands
*T*riumphantly

The matter of delighting daily and *triumphantly* keeps us in the cycle with increased momentum.

When we delight in the Lord we lift up our eyes with deliberate intent; it is a matter of the will, not the emotions. But it often refreshingly affects the emotions.

Paul tells us to be transformed by the renewing of our minds. Delighting in the Lord is a process; it's a practice and can become a splendid habit. Perhaps some of you are familiar with the painting "The Song of the Lark." It depicts a young gleaner, standing in the field with upturned face, her monotonous work forgotten for a brief moment as she listens to the musical call of a lark. That's what delighting in the Lord does; it is hearing His call in the midst of life's humdrum and responding with an upturned spirit of praise.

The dimension of delight is actually limitless; like circling ripples in a lake, it reaches to the very shores of heaven. There is a running-over quality about it, an effervescence, a prodigality that spills over into a divine certainty.

J. B. Phillips translates Romans 8:38, "I have become absolutely convinced that neither death nor life, neither messenger of Heaven nor monarch of earth, neither what happens today nor what may happen tomorrow, neither a power from on high nor a power from below, nor anything else in God's whole world has any power to separate us from the love of God in Christ Jesus our Lord!"[2]

What a joyous declaration of faith! *Faith* makes joy possible, not circumstances. The Center of our joy is Jesus Christ, the Son of God.

28

A detour along a highway implies that the regular direct route is closed. Our enemy seeks to place detour signs on the highway of holy living which say, "Take this roundabout way; deviate from the direct path." Detours from delight plunge us into the bumpy side road of fret and there is nothing to do but to back up, confess our need, and continue on the high road, blessing the Lord at all times, with His Word continually in our mouths.

I like the story of the Israelites given in 2 Chronicles, chapter 20. Singers were appointed who were to praise the Lord in the beauty of holiness. In verse 22 we read, "And when they began to sing and to praise, the Lord set ambushments against the children of Ammon . . . and they were smitten." Jehoshaphat would never have known victory from the enemy apart from these songs of praise. It is *our* best way, also, of overcoming our enemy. Delight is demonstrated in victory. After we cease our fretting, commit our way unto the Lord and trust in Him, we are able to rejoice in Him who "is the delight of our life as well as the life of our delight."

Delight is contagious. We can be carriers of the delight of the Lord. When I was a boy, our home was stricken with diphtheria and it was discovered that I was the culprit; I was the carrier of this disease. You know what our world needs? It needs Christians filled with delight exposing people to it wherever they go—in schools and hospitals, at desks, in garages and shops—people contagious for Christ. God wants us to be delightful Christians—delight-filled.

Unfortunately, one cannot get an injection of delight. The villagers in India never felt they had been properly treated by the doctor unless they received an injection. They could be given a handful of pills with explicit directions as to their use, but unless they got an injection they were not satisfied. But God's way is a handful of directives, and unless we follow Him explicitly, there can be no delight. It is through obedience that we discover joy. I like one scholar's definition of praise, "Inner health made audible." It is not an isolated experience; it is a way of life.

I find it best to keep short accounts with God. It is good to have a daily check during our devotions to see if we are delighting in the Lord. No hidden, unclean corners, no sweeping of life under the rug. (Too often this type of a rug gets pulled out from under us! It can be quite embarrassing.) Daily Everything Laid Into God's Hands Triumphantly—our finances, our mental life, our homelife, our business, our friends and associates. Nothing left out.

One translator uses for "delight" the word "relish." It implies something of a distinct flavor that we enjoy eating. What do you suppose David meant when he said, "O taste and see that the Lord is good"? His taste is not bitter and sour, but flavorful and sweet.

I wonder what our Master thinks when He looks into our shriveled hearts so lacking in praise and joyousness? It seems that we know everything about life in the Spirit except how to live it! With gracious understanding He would teach us how to live victoriously, that we might bear much fruit.

John Philip Sousa, known as "The March King," was surprised one day to hear floating up into his hotel room the strains of his favorite march, *The Stars and Stripes Forever.* It was being played in a slow, lazy, dragging manner by an organ grinder in the street below.

He dashed down into the street. "Here, here," he called to the sleepy organ grinder, "that is no way to play my march!"

He seized the handle and turned it vigorously. The music came out spirited and happy, and the little organ grinder smiled and bowed low to Mr. Sousa.

The next night Mr. Sousa heard his song again and this time the tempo was right. He looked out his window and noticed a large sign over the organ with the grinder's name on it and underneath the words, "Pupil of John Philip Sousa!"

If we ever learn to delight in the Lord—and we must—we shall write under the joys of our lives, "Pupil of Jesus Christ."

What about receiving the desires of our hearts? Strangely enough, before we learn this secret of delight we are inclined to think of all the things we would like to have; but after delight becomes a way of life, after we learn the secret of victorious living in the Spirit, our lives become uni-directional—we want most of all to be like Him and to live out His love for others. Everything else becomes a happy extra.

CHAPTER FIVE

Rest

While my family and I were vacationing in beautiful British Columbia we visited a special farm where Scottie dogs were trained to do all kinds of tricks. They were dressed up in children's clothes, made to jump through hoops, roll barrels, climb ladders, and do numerous things that dogs do not ordinarily do. The trainer always had a pocket filled with tidbits, and for every trick well done the dogs were rewarded with a word of encouragement and a tidbit. It was the old system of reward for disciplined performance. But the reward was never given until after the learning attempt was made.

Perhaps we move here from the ridiculous to the sublime, but there is a related point worthy of consideration. You may well ask me, "Why can't I go from commitment to rest? Why must I go through the full cycle of trust and delight?"

If we do not come the route of trust and delight we are hardly ready for the benefit of rest. Rest is usually hard-earned. The writer to the Hebrews admonishes, "Let us labour therefore to enter into that rest" (Heb. 4:11). Or, as *The Amplified Bible* says, "Let us therefore be zealous and exert ourselves and strive diligently to enter into that rest [of God]."[3] As the man who has come up the hard way in the financial world truly appreciates the value of money, so through obedience to personal disciplines do we know the real meaning of the word *rest*. There are divine patterns that must be followed or we cannot know the joy of "cashing in" on our investment in the Spirit.

This way of life is God's will for every child of His; it is not an option. He has designed a way for us, clear, direct, and attractive. It is to our advantage to follow instructions.

Sören Kierkegaard tells the story of a wild duck who decided to alter his pattern of life. As he was flying south with his fellow ducks he happened to see on the ground below him some corn a farmer had scattered for his barnyard fowls. So the lazy fellow fluttered down, joined the other ducks, ate the corn, and lingered on. Enjoying the food and security of the barnyard, he forgot about his flying companions and spent the winter in ease.

One spring day he heard the call of the wild ducks overhead as they were flying north. Something deep within him responded to the wild call and he tried to spread his wings. He fluttered up the best he could, but he had grown fat and flabby and could fly only as far as the eaves of the barn. He watched with despair as his former friends disappeared into the sky, leaving him earthbound to security.

This story is, too often, a description of our lives. We are made for personal victory in Christ Jesus. The plan is clear; the cycle is obvious. Yet we have allowed some deviation to destroy the call of the sky and have succumbed to living in "barnyard security," with wings helpless because of lack of use. This condition is not resting in the Lord; it is a condition of rusting in ourselves.

The rest I speak about is an active rest. He speaks; I listen and obey. And with each new situation I find my way through the cycle to inner rest. It is a rest from friction, not a rest from action. I like the words of Major Shupp of the Marine Corps, who years ago said, "If we can read it, we can do it." There is a rest in doing when it is in the Lord.

We should be sure to differentiate between *ease* and *rest*. Amos cries out, "Woe to them that are at ease in Zion" (6:1). Here is a picture of the barnyard duck. There is a great difference between comforts and comfort. People can live in ease but not experience rest. John D. Rockefeller was asked how much money it took to make a man happy. Speaking from experience he said, "Just a little bit more!" The rest God has for us enables us to abound in fruitful and tireless service to Him.

In Psalm 37, David reminds us to "rest in the Lord, and wait patiently for him" (37:7). The root from the Hebrew is "to cease, to be silent, or submit in silence to what He ordains." God has directives for us which cannot be received clearly until the inner station of the heart is quiet. The still, small voice may have something to say to us that will change our life's direction. We are never too old for this to

35

be a possibility; it keeps a stretch in the soul, the stretch of anticipation.

Because "yes" becomes the language of the heart we are able to live in relaxed readiness to God's will for our lives. A word of warning might be helpful here. We are talking about a cycle because life actually seems to move in cycles. It seems that we no sooner handle one problem or one situation than another one arises. The relationship is not disturbed because we know we are in Him, but the enemy tries with each new situation to bring in a spirit of fret. Repeatedly we turn from the possibility of fret to *commitment* of the new situation we are facing, *trusting* that He who has helped us thus far will continue to help and *praising* Him for victory. Thus we move back into a state of rest.

Perhaps it could be likened to the erratic flight pattern of a bird that flies in and up and around and back again in the process of getting food or protecting its mate or seeking a place to alight and sing. It's the nature of bird life to do this. Nor is our life static. It is ever in motion and thus always open to invasion, suggestion, temptation. But our "flight pattern" can always end in rest! That's the glorious truth.

> *My heart is resting, O my God;*
> *I will give thanks and sing.*
> *My heart is at the Secret Source*
> *Of every precious thing.*

It's the Secret Source to which we continually return and where we continually find rest.

When God gives us a directive, remember that

unbelief, or even doubt, can cause fret and get us out of the cycle. Phillips translates Hebrews 4:11: "Let us then be eager to know this rest for ourselves, and let us beware that no one misses it through falling into the same kind of unbelief."[2]

In verse 12, he says, "For the Word that God speaks is alive and active: it cuts more keenly than any two-edged sword: it strikes through to the place where soul and spirit meet, to the innermost intimacies of a man's being; it exposes the very thoughts and motives of a man's heart."[2]

Through relaxed readiness, the *r*'s of rest, comes a persistent spirit of faith. Unbelief keeps us from cashing in on our benefits; it is the great robber of that which God has prepared for us. Unbelief is a blinding sin.

This kind of rest I am writing about is creative rest; it consists of enthusiastic *expectation*. I think the young girl Rhoda, written about in Acts 12, had this kind of feeling. "Prayer was made without ceasing of the church unto God for him [Peter]" (Acts 12:5), but due to Rhoda's spirit of expectation she was able to hear the knock at the gate. (See Acts 12:13,14).

Probably the others were praying so loudly they could not hear the answer. Do we sometimes pray ourselves out of faith? It is quite possible. Although she left Peter standing at the gate without having even seen him, she knew his voice and believed in the answer to their prayers. Because of their incredulity, the disciples did not believe Rhoda, but "she constantly affirmed that it was even so" (Acts 12:15). She knew the *r*'s of rest in faith.

There is another prison story in Matthew's Gospel

which gives us a picture of how doubt can rob us of our rest. John the Baptist was imprisoned. Out of his dark, cold cell he sent a question to Jesus, "Are you the one who was to come or are we to look for somebody else?"[2] (Matt. 11:3). This was an honest query. John wanted to be sure; he was not experiencing unbelief.

How patient Jesus is with our questions! He did not rebuke John but gave this beautiful answer (also from Phillips' translation), "Go and tell John what you see and hear—that blind men are recovering their sight, cripples are walking, lepers being healed, the deaf hearing, the dead being brought back to life and the good news is being given to those in need. *And happy is the man who never loses his faith in me*"[2] (John 11:4-6).

These were not the words of a rebuke, but a loving message to the imprisoned, wondering, tempted John. Jesus does not rebuke honesty; He restores heart and a sense of expectation to such a one.

Rest not only means *readiness* and *expectation,* but also implies a steady *satisfaction.* The work of God's grace in sanctifying the believer has long been described as the establishing grace whereby one is established in God's rest and is satisfied for life to be this way. Paul was nearing the end of his earthly life and expressed his satisfaction with these words, "But none of these things move me, neither count I my life dear unto myself, so that I might finish my course with joy, and the ministry, which I have received of the Lord Jesus, to testify the gospel of the grace of God" (Acts 20:24). God's rest brings great inner poise.

In 1953 we returned to India for our second term. As I was elected field superintendent upon my return, I faced many important and far-reaching decisions. A month later I was scheduled to conduct the preachers' yearly meeting. It was a major project and I sincerely wanted God's plan for that gathering.

I set to work in prayer and preparation with true zeal. I had attended a rather large number of preachers' meetings and had a fair idea of what I wanted. But it seemed that every plan or idea turned into sawdust in my hands. I prayed all the more, for time was closing in on me. I needed assurance that His plans were mine. Or so I thought; actually I wanted to know that my plans were His.

In the midst of my frustration I gave myself to fasting as well as prayer. I searched God's Word for a special, divine signal or direction. Certainly Paul in Ephesians or Philippians would reveal a green light. But those great letters were like Sahara deserts to me. After a while my feverishness subsided and I quieted myself before the Lord. It was obvious that I was in the center and God had to get me out of the way. This took a bit of adjustment, for I did not realize what my problem was.

In a time of quiet meditation, God prompted me to read in Exodus, the area where I was having my regular Scripture reading. It was there in chapter 33 that I found my oasis. Moses was in a comparable situation. He was under the cloudy pillar in the Tabernacle and all the people were standing in their tent doors waiting for God's Word through him. Moses spoke with great boldness as he prayed, "Shew me now thy way" (33:13).

The startling answer God gave to Moses was my answer too. All the scaffolding of an intense feeling of personal responsibility went tumbling down as I read, "My presence shall go with thee, and I will give thee rest" (33:14).

His presence would go with me to the preachers' meeting. What more did I need? As I read the full passage I realized that *presence* and *rest* and *glory* were almost synonymous. My heart was swept with praise and thanksgiving as I placed everything completely into God's hands.

Out of that 1953 preachers' meeting came a glory of revival such as I have never experienced before or since. God's rest leads us to *triumph*, the *t* of the acrostic.

And there we have our definition for rest:

*R*eadiness
*E*xpectation
*S*atisfaction
*T*riumph

I want to close this chapter with a meaningful paraphrase of the Twenty-Third Psalm, published in *Guideposts*. It was entitled "23rd PSALM FOR BUSY PEOPLE."

The Lord is my Pacesetter; I shall not rush.
He makes me stop and rest for quiet intervals.
He provides me with images of stillness,
*   which restore my serenity.*
He leads me in ways of efficiency, through
*   calmness of mind,*
And His guidance is peace.

40

Even though I have a great many things
  to accomplish each day
I will not fret, for His presence is here.
His timelessness, His all-importance,
  will keep me in balance.
He prepares refreshment and renewal
  in the midst of my activity
By anointing my mind
  with His oils of tranquility.
My cup of joyous energy overflows.
Surely harmony and effectiveness shall be
  the fruits of my hours,
For I shall walk in the pace of my Lord,
  and dwell in His house forever.

                                    Toki Miyashina

CHAPTER SIX

A Rhythmic Pattern

With Jesus Christ as Lord and Center of our lives in this cycle of victorious living, we move into a very beautiful rhythmic pattern centering around Him and His will for us. This cycle is not an automatic thing that gets started and then goes on like wheels in a motor. It is made of flesh and bones and brain and heart moved by the winds of the Spirit in the surrendered heart. It is the relation of part to part and of parts to a whole. *Commit* is related to *trust, trust* to *delight, delight* to *rest,* all parts of the Author of Wholeness, Jesus Christ. Through the power of His Holy Spirit we have symmetry, balance and rhythm in our Christian living.

Let's think a bit about this matter of rhythm. There is in the body, I believe, a sense of rhythm which is health. A scientific term for it is *circadian rhythm,* my medical friends tell me. The body functions together as a happy, healthy unit. Sickness breaks this rhythm and makes one extremely uncomfortable, to say the least. And some illnesses are so serious they cause death and a cessation of all bodily rhythm.

Even so, fret can enter at any time making me feel very uncomfortable and, unless I see the problem and begin to handle it, all the spiritual balance in my life stops functioning until I face the situation, pray and seek divine help and again commit the matter or person unto the Lord! One of my parishioners said to me quite recently, "Pastor, *why* is the worst fret-trap of them all!"

The Scriptures abound in beautiful rhythmic expressions and promises. One of the most forceful is found in Genesis 8:22, God's promise to Noah after the flood:

> *"While the earth remaineth,*
> *seedtime and harvest,*
> *and cold and heat,*
> *and summer and winter,*
> *and day and night*
> *shall not cease."*

In the simplicity of these words lies the rhythm of the sunrise and the sunset, the rhythm of the tides and the moon, the revolving of the seasons, all the magnificence of God the Creator in divine patterns in His universe.

Another simple statement is used by Peter in the Book of Acts, chapter 10:38: "God anointed Jesus of Nazareth with the Holy Ghost and with power: who went about doing good . . . for God was with him."

"Who went about doing good"—the beauty of the rhythm of our Lord's life centering around His Father in heaven. He, our example, enables us to live even so in the power of His Spirit.

As you think about the cycle of victorious living you can almost hear the hum of a spinning wheel:

Commit—unto the Lord
Trust—in the Lord
Delight—in the Lord
Rest—in the Lord!

I firmly believe the fabric of life, the warp and woof of living, is found in this Thirty-Seventh Psalm.

Periodically, I get insight from the *Peanuts* cartoon. In one particular incident Sally is lying in bed with that funny look on her face that only Charles Schulz can draw. She says, "My alarm didn't go off."

She gets up and walks toward Charlie Brown who is holding a bowl of cereal in his hand. She holds up the alarm clock and says, "Maybe I wound it too tight. . . ."

"Sometimes if you wind an alarm clock too tight, it won't go off," she adds to the world in general.

Charlie walks over and sits in front of the TV. As he eats his cereal he mutters to himself, "We're all a little that way!"

Winding a clock too tight breaks the rhythmic ticking. It can break the mainspring. Taking ourselves too seriously does the same thing! I like the following definition for responsibility: my response-ability. And the greatest response-ability I have is to hand everything over to God with *no strings attached;* otherwise there is always the danger of tripping over the string.

Do you remember the fun of jumping rope? The whole game depended on the rhythmic turning of the rope and how carefully we gathered up our whole self and jumped into the center without dragging a foot. Does that say something to you?

When I read Paul's words in Philippians it's almost as though he had hold of one end of the rope and the Lord had the other as he wrote, "Rejoice in the Lord alway," and he keeps on turning the rope as he adds, "Again I say, Rejoice!" (Phil. 4:4).

"Be careful for nothing; but in everything by prayer and supplication with thanksgiving let your requests be made known unto God. And the peace of God, which passeth all understanding, shall keep your hearts and minds through Christ Jesus" (Phil. 4:6,7).

There is something about the grace of God that puts rhythm into our lives. Hear it in this verse, "If we walk in the light, as he is in the light, we have fellowship one with another, and the blood of Jesus Christ his Son cleanseth us from all sin" (1 John 1:7). What rhythm! A good walker paces himself into a pattern of sheer enjoyment and everything he sees adds to his joy: flowers, mountains, birds, streams—or even cars and people and city lawns! We have fellowship and are kindred spirits with all mankind and nature. Walking in the light, the beautiful light of God.

I was clearing my luggage on the docks of Bombay back in 1952 when, to my amazement, I saw one of the huge freight cars being moved along the tracks not by an engine but by twenty thin coolies. As I watched I could hear a low rhythmic chant as they leaned forward, chanted, rested, leaned again and pushed, doing the seemingly impossible in one mighty unified effort bound together with song.

There are rhythms that help us to "draw on our innermost." Such is the work of grace in our hearts in sunshine or shadow, joy or sorrow. When sorrow strikes us we cry out with George Herbert,

"Who would have thought my shrivelled heart could have recovered greenness?"

But the rhythm of life moves on, thank God, and spring comes again after a cold, barren winter.

There are many sayings ascribed to Jesus which are not written in the Gospels. One of these statements has a deep truth in it—"Turn over any stone, and I am there." No matter how hard the situation, nor how far-out the territory, Jesus is "always previous!"

Let us suppose you have been living victoriously and due to a catastrophe the sun is blotted out; you feel you've lost your way. Where to start? Where to turn? I know no better answer than to *do the next thing* that has to be done. It will probably be something small and menial like fixing a meal, washing a window, making a bed, driving your car to work, facing "faceless" people. Just keep on turning over the stones as you come to them. You'll find Him there . . . and there . . . and there. For He promised, "I will never leave you." (See Heb. 13:5.) Continue to keep the first thrust of the cycle in operation, *Commit.*

"Why did it happen to me?" Commit!

"There is no fair play in life!" Commit!

"I've always tried to obey God; what did I do wrong?" Commit!

"It doesn't pay to take up your cross; everything is topsy-turvy." Commit!

"But He *said* that no good thing would He withhold from them that walk uprightly." (See Ps. 84:11.) Commit. Trust.

"Help me, God. I've lost my way. I'm out of joint with Thee and Thy will." *Commit. Trust. Delight.* In the Lord . . .

"Thank You, Jesus. By faith I know You are there. Yes, for *this* I have Jesus." Commit. Trust. Delight. Rest. Rest? Yes, rest in the Lord. And the old freight train begins to move down the tracks. The jump rope begins to turn. The spinning wheel starts to hum. I find from the wound of grace comes the rhythm of grace. And I *keep on doing the next thing* in the name of Christ, redemptively.

The most difficult experience in life to find our way through is sorrow. A deep undercurrent of sorrow is a part of living for all of us; sooner or later, our hearts break. Jeremiah writes ". . . there is sorrow on the sea; it cannot be quiet" (Jer. 49:23). The dictionary defines sorrow as "the deep, often long-continued mental anguish caused by a sense of loss, disappointment, remorse or regret."

There is a strange rhythm in sorrow; tides of suffering move in and out of our lives. At sorrow's full tide it is good to at least know where the answer lies! To know that in the darkness the Lord is standing by whether we can see Him or not. And one day, even as tides recede, so the rhythm of release begins as we place the entire sorrow into the nail-pierced hands of the One who understands. "Surely he hath borne our griefs, and carried our sorrows" (Isa. 53:4).

No doubt you ask me, "How can delight meet my need at such a time?"

I feel the answer once again is found in the Word of God in Hebrews 13:15: "By him therefore let us offer the sacrifice of praise to God continually. . . ." It is a very divine privilege to share in the sufferings of Christ, thus making our sorrow redemptive. Our delight comes from the awareness that we are being conformed into His image!

If sorrow becomes redemptive we are then able to move out and "to comfort them which are in any trouble, by the comfort wherewith we ourselves are comforted of God" (2 Cor. 1:4). Our Lord knew the underside of suffering. One day on a hillside He looked upon the multitudes with compassion as He said, "Blessed are they that mourn: for they shall be comforted" (Matt. 5:4). Is there any comfort quite so healing as to be able, once again, to reach out and touch our brother's need?

A young man stricken with a fatal illness, was writing to a friend about the short time he had left to live. In his letter he expressed his firm faith with these words, "God's love is deeper than the deepest sea and it has no ebb or flow." What confidence!

In order to have true rhythm there has to be a constant. An absolute. Such is the great love of God. He is always there and in Him there is no variableness nor shadow of turning!

The cycle of victorious living revolves around the love of God. That is where the rhythm begins, out of the heart of God, and that is where it returns.

CHAPTER SEVEN

Jesus Is Lord

During the wonderful outpouring of the Holy Spirit in revival in India in 1954, my wife and I were asked to share our experiences with another denomination in the north of India. We were invited to a well-known hospital compound in Vrindaban, a city where there are as many idols as people. From the very first meeting, the winds of the Spirit began to blow. People were gripped by a spirit of openness and honesty, and prayers of many years were answered.

One afternoon I sat in the old mission bungalow with Mr. C——, a fine Indian Christian, a converted Hindu and a Sanskrit scholar. There was an air of brooding about him as he rocked back and forth in a hand-carved rocker. The more we discussed things of the Spirit, the more I sensed his deep dissatisfaction. He had come with a need.

After a few minutes he leaned forward and looked at me intently.

"Mr. Lee," he said, "I want you to tell me what total freedom means. I don't want your answer today; I want you to think about it and to pray about it. But God has told me that you can give me the answer I need."

I was quite astonished. I promised him I would certainly pray about it and mind the Spirit. I went to our room feeling mystified and a bit troubled. What could I tell this great scholar? But I quickly realized it would not be I; it would be Christ.

Two days later we returned to the historic old parlor in which he had found Christ years before. (He was converted through reading the Bible.) With a look of anticipation, he sat down in the same old rocking chair.

I waited a bit before speaking. Finally I said, "The answer seems so simple I am hesitant to give it; yet I feel it is from the Lord."

"I know it is from the Lord," he promptly replied. "Let's hear it. I'm ready."

"Well, it's simply this: If the Son makes you free, you are free indeed and that means freedom *in* things, not freedom *from* things."

He closed his eyes, leaned back in his chair for a few seconds, then said, "Say that again."

"God wants to free you where you are, not take you out of the situation," I replied.

"Say it once again."

I repeated the thought.

With tears filling his dark brown eyes, he reached over and placed my big hand in his strong brown hands and said, "I accept it. That's the truth I need:

freedom *in* things, not freedom *from* things. Thank you."

He arose from the chair and with a look of peace said, "I'll do it. I'll accept what must be accepted and find my freedom right where I am." He walked from the room with determination.

He said nothing more to me at the time and I left the room thoroughly mystified. Later on I discovered how beautifully the Holy Spirit had guided. This man was embroiled in a delicate and difficult family situation from which there was no escape. God showed him the escape was within himself, in his attitude toward the situation. Through a marvelous series of events, God worked things out beyond our asking or thinking.

The entire week was a week of miracles. When it came time to leave, Mr. C—— rode with me in a horse-drawn tonga to the station. We shared the rich experiences of the week. Our fellowship in Christ was very warm. The train was approaching the station and we were in the process of giving luggage to the coolies when he turned to me rather abruptly and said, "Do you know what *'Jesus is Lord'* really means?"

Sensing he wanted a negative answer, I told him I did not know.

"Well, *'Jesus is Lord'* means He is my Owner; He is my Possessor." And with a hearty slap on my shoulder he added, "He is my Dispossessor!"

As he spoke, the train roared in, coolies grabbed the luggage and I had very little time to reply. I thanked him warmly and we waved good-bye.

Later in the night I thought about what he had

said to me. *"Jesus is Lord"* is a phrase E. Stanley Jones used over and over again with three fingers held high. Mr. C—— was giving names to those three fingers: Owner . . . Possessor . . . Dispossessor.

I recalled the words of Job, "The Lord gave, and the *Lord hath taken away;* blessed be the name of the Lord" (1:21).

Job's testimony came after he had lost everything dear to him. He suffered bereavement and questions and misunderstanding and bodily pain. But he blessed the name of the Lord, who, though He had dispossessed him of all he had, had not disinherited him. The thing that mattered most remained—his relationship with his God.

I wondered what God had removed from this Indian scholar to make him free. I never actually knew, but later he wrote a postscript to his well-known autobiography, telling about his newfound freedom in the Spirit. That was answer enough!

Jesus is Lord is the great center of the cycle of victorious living. The key phrase from each of these four verses in Psalm 37 is *"in the Lord."* "Commit thy way *unto the Lord";* "Trust *in the Lord";* "Delight . . . *in the Lord";* "Rest *in the Lord."* This kind of living demands a sacramental view of life where everything is done unto the Lord. All our being, as well as our doing, must answer the question: "Is Jesus Christ the Center?" Not that we might feel better or work more effectively, but that in all things He might have the glory.

E. Stanley Jones said that either Jesus is Lord *of all* or He is not Lord *at all.* Too often we give the testimony, "Jesus means everything to me," when all

54

the time someone else or something else is at the center of our lives. The center must be right or everything else is off balance. If we miss this truth we miss everything. No matter how good our center may be, *if it is other than Jesus Christ,* it is not good enough. Remember, our center controls us, as the hub controls the wheel. He is "the summing up of all that man needs."

Jesus is Lord was the creed of the Early Church, and since the Resurrection it is the great recurring theme in the symphony of the Kingdom of God.

The generation of today asks, "What difference does it make? What difference does it make that Jesus is Lord?"

If Jesus is Lord, life has meaning. He makes the difference between victory and defeat, between hope and despair, between life and death.

Too many circles of philosophical thought end in a "horror of darkness." Inability to communicate is one of the great problems of existentialism. Like a figure in a nightmare, man wants to cry out, but he has no voice. Jesus Christ gives us a voice, a purpose, a center by *being* the Voice, the Purpose, the Center. He makes all the difference in the world.

The rich young man, pressed in by life, came running up to Jesus to ask, "Good Master, what shall I do that I may inherit eternal life?" (Mark 10:17). He was sincere; he was troubled; he really wanted an answer.

Jesus loved him as He looked on him, and longed for him to fulfill his personhood. But the young man lacked one thing, allegiance to Christ, which would mean cutting off from all his earthly supports. Christ placed His finger on the vulnerable spot as He said, "Go . . . sell . . . give . . . and come, take up the cross, and follow me" (Mark 10:21). The young man turned away sorrowful. His center controlled him and his center was self. The words of Christ were action words, words demanding a reversal of direction. They were words that spelled a cross.

If we were to draw a line vertically and one horizontally through the center of our diagram, we would form a cross. At that point we find Jesus Christ. Everything we *commit* is committed to the Cross; our *trust* is wholly in the Cross; our *delight* is in the Cross, as Paul said in Galatians 6:14, "But God forbid that I should glory, save in the cross of our Lord Jesus Christ, by whom the world is crucified unto me, and I unto the world."

And our *rest*, too, is in the finished work of Christ on the Cross, for every day we experience something of the death of Jesus, so that we may also know the power of the life of Jesus in these bodies of ours.

It is through Him that "we live, and move, and *have our being*" (Acts 17:28). He gets into our personalities, our hang-ups, our subconscious, our needy selves and creates a growing edge that continues until life is over. We are ever discovering our potential in Him and moving in a "divine crescendo" more and more to the perfect day. He heals wounds, and is continually helping us with our infirmities, our complexes, our "maladjustive impulses," our "damaged emotions."

Romans 8:11 says, "Once the Spirit of him who raised Christ Jesus from the dead lives within you he will, by that same Spirit, bring to your whole being new strength and vitality."[2] The Holy Spirit is the greatest creative force in the world.

He guides us in our interpersonal relationships. When Jesus is Lord, He controls our friendships, our attitudes, our activities. Peter was quite disturbed about John. Perhaps he was smarting a bit after his soul searching on the beach. However, he said to Christ, "Lord, and what shall this man do?" (John 21:21).

Phillips translates Christ's answer, "If it is my wish for him to stay until I come, is that your business, Peter? You must follow me"[2] (John 21:22).

That puts an end to many unsettling matters. "You must follow me." Any attitude, any liaison, any transaction that keeps us from following Christ is "out of bounds" to us. *Jesus is Lord* leads through a narrow path to life eternal. There is not room for a great deal of impedimenta.

Who knows better than the Holy Spirit how infirm we are? It is our handful of dust with which He is constantly at work! J. B. Phillips translates 2 Corinthians 4:7,5, "This priceless treasure we hold, so to speak, in a common earthenware jar—to show that the splendid power of it belongs to God and not to us. . . . For it is Christ Jesus as Lord whom we preach, not ourselves."[2]

In an age of humanism, the Spirit would teach us that He is Host of this universe and we are His guests. But He allows us to "carry around" this great treasure in our homely selves, that we might ever be reminded of our dependence on our God.

What difference does it make? Listen to these words further on, "We are handicapped on all sides, but we are never frustrated; we are puzzled, but never in despair. We are persecuted, but we never have to stand it alone: we may be knocked down but we are never knocked out!"[2] (2 Cor. 4:8,9). He gives us the ability to keep on going in His power.

I well remember an experience I had several years ago. I sat down to an evening meal with my family as though it were a parenthesis to more important things. During the meal, I was somewhat preoccupied. All of a sudden my younger son said, "Dad, do you really have to go out again tonight?"

His question cut into my thinking like a knife. No, I really did not *have* to go calling that night. I decided right then that the most important thing for me that evening was to remain at home with my family. It was a great relief to quit spinning my wheels, have a relaxed spirit, and enjoy the ones I love. The kingdom would go on, for *Jesus* is Lord, not I!

The cycle of victorious living requires a teachable spirit. In this way we cultivate a heart "at leisure from itself"; we have an inner poise and security from which we fulfill Christ's command to *go*, to *tell*, to *do*.

When Jesus is Lord we know the deep meaning of the hymn:

> *In service which Thy love appoints*
> *There are no bonds for me;*
> *My secret heart is taught the truth*
> *That makes Thy children free;*
> *A life of self-renouncing love*
> *Is one of liberty.*
>
> —A. L. Waring

So, now we move on and the adventure of life in the cycle never ends. There will be new insights, new joys, new discoveries; for, really, this total concept is only my way of describing our walk with Jesus Christ. It is life on tiptoes of excitement in the Spirit.

May I say to you, "Have a great time in *your* adventure IN Christ, in *The Cycle of Victorious Living.*"

Someday we shall talk it over together with our wonderful Lord, who is the Center of everything; for "he is before all things, and by him all things consist. And he is the head of the body, the church: who is the beginning, the firstborn from the dead; that in all things he might have the preeminence. For it pleased the Father that in him should all fulness dwell" (Col. 1:17-19).

Jesus is Lord!

CHAPTER EIGHT

It Works

What father has not sat down with his son with a new toy that needs assembling and said, "Now, let's see, if we follow these directions, I'm sure we'll find out how it works"? Then painstakingly he reads the directions, allowing the boy to do as much of the work as he can. After a time of patience and cooperation they go outdoors and fly the kite or float the boat or watch the airplane zoom into loops around the backyard. Then the little fellow cries excitedly, "Boy, Dad, we really made it work!"

I would be wasting your time and mine if I were advocating a way of life that did not work. In this book I have tried to give a set of instructions as guidelines to victorious living. I have probably used a new avenue of approach, but it is the same grand, old truth. The testimony of scores of individuals has convinced me it works; it opens the way to a new level of sanctified living.

There are many ways a minister earns his right to share in the lives of his people. Quite often an illuminating truth from the pulpit becomes a passport to a new area of Christian life. Such is this message on the cycle of victorious living which, because of the response, I preach once a year in my present pulpit.

In a former pastorate there was a little lady in the congregation who came faithfully on Sunday mornings but, because of ill health, was unable to attend other services. She had been widowed for a number of years. While her husband was alive he had almost wrapped her in tissue paper as he tenderly cared for her every need. After his death she had kept going, but on a very slight margin.

She supplied our home with her special brand of jams and jellies. Not long after I had preached my sermon on the cycle of victorious living, I decided our jam supply was low, so stopped by her home one warm, spring day. As I stepped up to her porch I could hardly believe my ears. She was playing the piano and singing a hymn with great gusto. I knocked lightly, as I did not want to disturb her; yet I was extremely curious as to this joyful sound coming from her usually silent house.

I waited until she had finished a verse and then knocked louder. She came to the door with the glow of the music still on her face.

"Why, Sister _____," I said in amazement, "I did not know you could sing and play so well. I really enjoyed that!"

"Come in, Pastor, and I'll tell you what has happened to me," she replied as she swung open the door.

I walked into her humble little home and sat near the piano as she shared her experience with me.

"After you preached your sermon on 'the cycle' I knew there was something in that sermon for me. Since my husband died I have gone on living, but more as an existence. New truth has come through to me and now I'm really *alive!*"

She whirled around on the piano stool and we sang a duet of joy together. Oh, yes, I got my jars of jelly but no gift was so great as this heart-warming testimony.

Her health did not improve appreciably. In fact, in a subsequent examination her doctor told her he could not see what was keeping her alive. But she confided in me that everything was committed to the Lord, that she was delighting in "the cycle" and that was reason enough to live.

Since writing of this experience I have received a note from this woman in which she said, in part:

". . . the messages you gave, Brother Lee, on the Thirty-Seventh Psalm still linger with me. Today is the second time I have been out to church since Christmas but through all the pain and suffering the blessed words linger with me, 'Heaven will be worth it all . . .'"

Once the truth of this cycle becomes a way of life, it goes on and on through the years, come what may.

Ministers, like doctors, hear from parishioners or patients at odd times and in unexpected places. Mrs.

Lee and I had been asked to speak at a valentine banquet in a neighboring church. It was enjoyable sharing our thoughts with young people—thoughts on love and marriage and compatibility. After the banquet a young woman came up to me and said, "Let me tell you, Brother Lee, that cycle of victorious living really works!"

I was a bit startled to hear this enthusiastic testimony in this port city where I thought I knew no one. "Now, where did you hear that?" I asked, quite puzzled.

She opened her Bible where she had especially marked Psalm 37 and reminded me of an indoor camp meeting held in Norwalk, California, where I was the speaker.

"You pulled out a large blackboard and drew the cycle on it and then proceeded to tell us how to live victoriously. I made up my mind that I had better get started in the cycle. That was six months ago and my life has been completely changed ever since!"

The best part of that banquet for me was to see this woman's radiant face and to share in her joy as she reached a new level of Spirit-filled living.

A friend and I had spent many hours together as we prayed and believed for his spiritual release. The cycle had been a prominent part of our times of sharing. Through God's Word and especially through Psalm 37, he had found many answers for his badly shattered life.

In trying to find his way he had wisely sought professional help.

One day during our regular visits he surprised me

with an account of his most recent session with his doctor. "Believe it or not, Pastor, I took along this little diagram of the cycle and showed it to my doctor."

I was surprised, naturally. Most patients would not have this much courage! "What did he think?" I asked.

"The doctor looked at the cycle as I explained it to him and what it had done for me and he said, 'This truth is psychologically sound and seems to be a great answer.'

"Then I smiled as I quietly told him the whole principle was found in the Bible, in the Thirty-Seventh Psalm!"

I walked into a hospital room where a teen-ager was lying flat on her back with a broken leg hoisted up in a splint. An arm also was broken and her head was severely lacerated. I prayed a prayer of thanksgiving that this young lady was alive, as the car in which she had been riding had been hit by a train and the young driver had been killed. She was a new convert and radiant in her new-found faith.

Several days later I returned to see her, and several of her church friends were in the room with her. I walked over to her bed to pray with her, and as I turned, my attention was drawn to something hanging above her door. There, staring her right in the face, was the diagram of the cycle of victorious living which one of her friends had drawn for her.

"Linda," they had said to her, "this is what you need more than anything else, right now!"

And with youthful candor she admitted it was true

as she added, "Pastor, it has lifted my spirits totally and taken my mind off myself. It is the best prescription of all!"

In order to keep in touch with people in my congregation I have designed a *Friendship in Worship* card. One of the request categories on it states: *Appointment with the Pastor.* One Monday as I was going over these cards, I noticed a young veteran from Vietnam had checked the box for an appointment.

Later that week he sat across my desk from me, completely weighed down with burdens of home and family and adjustments that only war veterans would understand. I let him fully unload and then asked him if he was familiar with the cycle of victorious living. As it was new to him, I took out a small card on which the diagram was printed and shared it with him. Then I said, "Have you been filled with the Holy Spirit?"

He was silent for a few seconds. He had been brought up in the church and was almost delighting in some of his "hang-ups." He had learned a commanded discipline in the army, but when on his own, spiritually, he found himself extremely undisciplined.

"No, Pastor, I don't believe I have ever asked the Holy Spirit to take over the center of my life. I have been the center," he said quite candidly.

We looked over the cycle again and I showed him what it meant for Jesus Christ to be Lord of one's life. Self had to be crucified in order for Christ to be Lord. A deliberate transaction was necessary.

Light came to him. He accepted it and prayed a prayer of surrender to the Holy Spirit, confessing his need. Of course the Holy Spirit came, and the man left my office delighting in the Lord.

A few days later I met him again after the close of a service. He gripped my hand warmly as he said, "Pastor, it works!" I will soon be performing his marriage ceremony, and what a different start his new life will have as he lives in the cycle of victorious living!

Not too long ago I was invited to lunch with a fine member of my church who wished to discuss a means of outreach in his community. It was a stimulating time for both of us.

On our way home I asked him about an automobile accident that he had been involved in the week before. His brand-new car had been demolished. It was a miracle the man was alive.

"Were you wearing your seat belt?" I asked.

"I sure was!" he answered. "But let me tell you how that cycle of victorious living you preach about helped me in that nearly fatal accident. After the impact, I skidded across the intersection and as I came to a stop I realized I was apparently not seriously injured but my shiny new car was a wreck. In those first stunned seconds I found myself committing the entire situation to the Lord with a calmness that could come only from the Divine.

"In fact, I was so calm I was able to help the other man involved make out his report. He was greatly upset and nervous. The next day I called at his home to see how he was and helped him with more paper work. He looked at me in amazement as he asked,

'Why are you doing this for me? You have every reason to be doing just the opposite!'

"Then in a flash came the opportunity to explain to this man what Jesus Christ and His peace meant to me. And, Pastor," he added, "the cycle was there in my mind the moment I needed it and I never had a fretful minute during that entire experience!"

Perhaps this is what Will Huff meant when he talked about "nick-of-time grace." Anyway, it works!

The last example I want to share with you in this chapter concerns a man I have never met. The fact is, he lived six hundred years before Christ was born. His name was Habakkuk. He looked about and saw the oppression of his people; he looked up and saw the inscrutability of his God; he looked within and saw a living faith. Like David, his faith was his hope in this evil world.

The last three verses of this little book contain some of the most magnificent imaginative poetry in literature. They also constitute one of the strongest declarations of faith ever written—a moving testimony of the cycle of victorious living:

Although the fig tree shall not blossom,
neither shall fruit be in the vines;
the labour of the olive shall fail,
and the fields shall yield no meat;
the flock shall be cut off from the fold,
and there shall be no herd in the stalls:
Yet I will rejoice in the Lord,
I will joy in the God of my salvation.
The Lord God is my strength,

and he will make my feet like hinds' feet,
and he will make me to walk
upon mine high places (Hab. 3:17-19).

The Lord God not only gives strength; He *is* strength. As we *commit, trust, delight,* and *rest* in the Lord, we are enabled to leap up into the heights of God's grace and love, sharing in the heavenly places with our Lord Jesus Christ, "far above all principality, and power, and might, and dominion, and every name that is named, not only in this world, but also in that which is to come" (Eph. 1:21).

CHAPTER NINE

Recycled Lives

Since this book was first written I have had the joy of hearing from many people, either by letter or word of mouth, that they have found this truth— this cycle of victorious living—a sound working principle in their lives. In this chapter I want to share excerpts from these letters.

Early one morning we received a long distance call from a young college professor's wife in the Midwest. She asked for a special prayer from our prayer group that meets from 6:00 to 7:00 A.M. each Friday. She had recently had her first baby, a little son. The delivery was difficult and his little arm had been injured. She herself was extremely weak and unable to care for her baby. She needed help desperately. We prayed with her over the telephone and later the prayer group prayed for her.

About a week later we received a letter from her. Here are excerpts from the letter:

"This has been an extremely difficult week of testing, but God has been close through it all. God has taught me more about the cycle of victorious living this week than I have ever experienced before."

But after she called us, things seemed to go from bad to worse, as is often the case.

She continues to write, "Later in the day I had another setback and so a little wedge of doubt crept in, but I decided to really seriously try rejoicing no matter how bad things got. I decided to be very literally thankful for strength for each moment and hour, and to make myself not think or worry about the next day.

"I sang all the songs I could think of while I held the baby and thought the words while lying down. I kept hoping soon I would be better. But Saturday I was much worse (with other complications) and this continued through Monday. Tuesday—I felt miraculously better. Today I am maintaining strength.

"But the blessing has come in trusting God moment by moment. As I praise Him for *everything*, pain and weakness as well as strength, I have found peace. I still find myself fretting all too often, but when I realize it, I start committing the situation to God again and trusting Him! though I still am in the process of learning patience."

Then she adds, "Stevie (the baby) is doing much better. Much of the swelling has gone from his arm and shoulder. His hand has a strong grip now and he moves his arm on his own—he is such a good baby and does not fuss very much at all."

After reading this letter, I felt most grateful to God that when we are learning our lessons of trust He does not weary of our *oft-comings!* There are no limits to grace. "He giveth and giveth and giveth again."

I am very aware of the fact that among those listening to me preach there are many who stagger under crushing loads.

Into my congregation one morning came such a visitor on whom life had caved in. But through the message, the Holy Spirit spoke to this suffering woman, and in a few days she came to my office for a talk. Her situation was full of heartache. After twenty-five years of a compatible marriage her husband walked off saying, "It's all over." She felt as if a tornado had roared through the main street of her life and there was nothing left but wreckage. Now she was out working for the first time in her life. A small, inadequate apartment had taken the place of her spacious home near the ocean.

The more I listened, the more helpless I felt as she poured out her sorrow that afternoon. I shared the cycle of victorious living with her, using the diagram I keep on my desk. This diagram is embroidered on linen by a young woman who found it meaningful in her life and shared her joy with me by this priceless gift. I prayed with my visitor and gave her a copy of my book to read and pray about.

In the process of time I received an encouraging letter from her. While she was ironing one day she listened to a sermon-tape on victorious living. She writes:

". . . the Holy Spirit came through that tape right

into my life. Tears flowed and I began then and there by God's help to start living a victorious Christian life. The Lord speaking to me through your message turned me right around. Thanks to His grace towards me this life is so changed.

"I am cheerful. This had to be the Lord's work as the psychologist failed and the church had failed to make me happy with my life as I had to face it every day.

"There is truly a peace that passeth understanding. I am now able to accept life's heartache and struggle.

"Trust. Commit. These are real tangible things to me . . . not just words. I recall walking out on the pier by the beach and looking out over the water, watching the sea gulls, and there by the ocean (where I always feel so close to God) giving my son back to God. This heartbreaking experience meant seeing my beautiful son taken away in handcuffs. He met a dedicated chaplain who led him to the Lord; but I first had to say, 'Lord, here is this boy, I take my hands off him and give him back to You.'

"It took me a little longer to give up my husband and that house.

"There's no way to tell you how things have changed: a good job, a new car, wonderful working conditions, many new friends, self-respect, goals.

"Now, at fifty-four years of age, I'm finding life more interesting and exciting every day."

Thank God for the seed that drops quietly in the heart and brings so rich a harvest.

A young man in my congregation wrote me to report on how his first month of total commitment had gone. In one paragraph of this exciting letter he writes:

"The following Monday after I really committed my life to Him the devil really played havoc with my thoughts. I wasn't going to give up this time. I sat at my desk at 8:45 and laid my hands palms down on this desk, where I am sitting now, and prayed for strength. Then I turned my hands over and closed my fingers tightly and asked the Lord to give me a Scripture verse. I opened my Bible and He gave me the whole seventeenth chapter of John!

"My discouragement left me and I immediately felt the presence of the Holy Spirit near me. My Bible reading and my prayer-life has grown, and my walk with Jesus is stronger each day."

Another time I was extremely pleased to hear from an administrative assistant who had charge of sending many college young people to various parts of the world to assist in missionary work. He wrote, "I wanted to let you know that your *Cycle of Victorious Living* was one of the big topics of conversation this year. So often it was referred to by various students and many felt it was a key to their own attitudes towards this summer's activities.

"We had our Language Training south of Mexico City, and on Sunday the fifty involved in Spanish Language Training were sent to churches in Mexico City. I know of at least one fellow who was asked to preach unexpectedly and shared your message on *The Cycle of Victorious Living!* He said the response was very positive.

"I just thought this word might give you a gleam

of encouragement as your ministry and influence disburses in so many different places."

I think the thing which pleased me most was the fact that this pattern of living appealed to young people.

Another inspiring letter:

"God bless you for sharing *The Cycle of Victorious Living*. Please send me a chart depicting it so I can teach it in my Junior Department opening assembly!

"A year ago I fell and broke my back. I had to lie flat. Over and over I played your tapes. I couldn't look anywhere but straight up into the face of God. What a blessing that broken back turned out to be. Through bitter tears of bewilderment I began to deliberately thank God for this broken back—for every problem and tragedy that was in my life. I began to praise Him for His great purposes and His thoughts that are above my thoughts; for His love for me and His capability to solve every one of these hideous, impossible problems! I gave myself anew to Him.

"Well, the miracles started happening and they haven't stopped since. Our marriage has never been better; our rebellious daughter accepted Christ, and God has given her a Christian husband and they are both in college making top grades.

"And time would fail me to tell you how God has blessed mentally, socially, spiritually, physically and financially. In every conceivable way blessing upon blessing has been heaped upon us. He picked up all my burdens and then He did a very lovely, unexpected thing—He reached over and scooped me up too, broken body and all, and carried me! What a Saviour!"

A young minister wrote thanking me for what the cycle had meant to his life, helping him through various crises. He found particular help through the thought of "commitment—hands down." Then he adds:

"As I worked through the 'Cycle of Victorious Living' I noticed a cycle of defeat that was made up of opposites to the cycle of victory. I share it with you:

Cycle of Victory	Cycle of Defeat
Fret not	Fret—destructive worry
Commit—hands down	Reservations about God's will
Trust—lean hard	Self-centeredness
Delight—the joy of looking up	Complaint—verbal bitterness
Rest—in the Lord	Restlessness of spirit

"Again my thanks for the help your message has given me."

Many other people have also shared similar thoughts with me of their own personal insights through this truth which prove the Holy Spirit is guarding His revelation. It is not mine.

The last letter I wish to share with you is from a missionary nurse. Actually, it is a summary of a correspondence we have had, centering around the cycle pattern. She writes:

"Yesterday I started re-reading your book on *The Cycle of Victorious Living* and hit a hang-up that has not yet been resolved. Why is it that it is so hard sometimes to really commit a question to the Lord? It doesn't take much, does it? Just one uncommitted area and all relationships begin to go sour. I have argued with myself and God for hours. I've tried and failed so many times in the past eight months.

"It is fret, isn't it? That can be such a vicious cycle."

She describes the problem and then continues:

"But a list of the symptoms doesn't help much, for the real problem is that I have not committed an uncertain future of my missionary nursing career to Christ and left it there. The doubts and fears are legion. I feel guilty because they are there and as a result my fellowship with the Lord is not what it should be.

"Excuses are legion, too! And there is another problem! As I listened to one of your sermons last week, I realized again that I must now really believe that God's love and forgiveness is for me, for I let my sense of guilt and failure separate me from Him until prayer becomes just a duty . . .

"You said it was a matter of the will, didn't you? OK. I *will*, hands open and palms down, give the Lord the past failures, the present frustrations and the future fears! What a relief!

"You know what I'm thinking of now? When we have heavy rains, the dirt and debris come down the river and pile up at the mouth of the intake of our hydrowater race. Before long the flow of water is cut down and there is not enough water power to generate the needed electricity for the station. Right now with the commitment made, the channel is open and God's Spirit can pour His love through me to those patients that I will soon be caring for—and to the many others that I will have contact with tonight."

In a later progress report she writes:

"The battle has been fought in stages, thanks to the Lord's understanding that I probably could not have taken it all at once. The last battle was fought this week—and the Lord has given wonderful victory and peace. I have been fighting for the responsibility and authority that I felt should be mine . . . I needed to give up my 'rights' and the surrender brought victory. It is strange, isn't it, that the ones who surrender are the ones who really win the battle!

". . . 'the less I have, the more I depend on Him' . . . those words have brought real victory as I have gone back to them time and time again in this time of beginning to learn to be thankful for all things. It started by really being able to thank the Lord—and mean it—for my total inability to do anything in my own strength. I realized that I didn't have to be independent, for I could depend on Him. Words can't explain the transformation that the Lord has brought.

"So I began to say 'thank You, Jesus' for things around the house, gifts, rich friendships and experiences around the world. Big things and little frustrating things all were brought into this new concept of thankfulness as the Lord worked in my heart.

"There are so many things to praise the Lord for, but near the top of the list of items for praise is the way the Lord has changed my attitude toward my work in the hospital. I guess the only way to adequately express that change is to say that God has given such deep assurance that the work I am doing is His will for me right now. There is a deep restful peace within myself. Fits the cycle, doesn't it?"

This sampling of sharing the working of the Holy Spirit in the lives of others makes me say with the song writer, "To God be the glory; great things He hath done!"

Dare I close this chapter with another one of my illustrations from *Peanuts?*

Charlie Brown is walking away from Linus as Linus says, "Thank you—I'll try to do what you suggested."

He sees Lucy and says to her, "Charlie Brown just gave me some advice . . ."

"Did you understand it?"

"Of course I understood it!"

Lucy turns on her heel as she answers, "Never take any advice that you can understand . . . it can't possibly be any good!"